DISCOVERING ANCIENT ROME

EXPLORING ANCIENT CIVILIZATIONS

DISCOVERING ANCIENT ROME

SAMUEL WILLARD CROMPTON

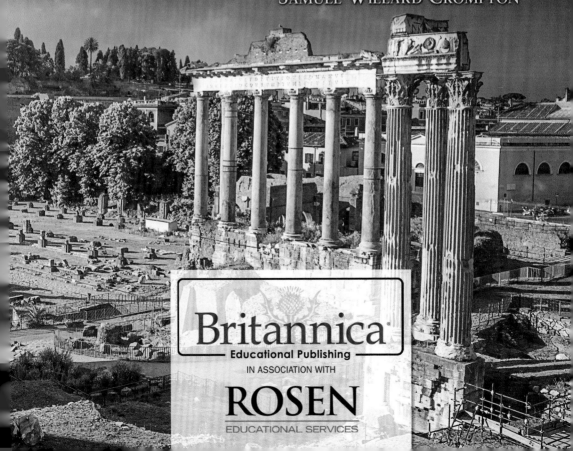

Britannica®

Educational Publishing

IN ASSOCIATION WITH

ROSEN

EDUCATIONAL SERVICES

Published in 2015 by Britannica Educational Publishing (a trademark of Encyclopædia Britannica, Inc.) in association with The Rosen Publishing Group, Inc.
29 East 21st Street, New York, NY 10010

Distributed exclusively by Rosen Publishing.
To see additional Britannica Educational Publishing titles, go to rosenpublishing.com.

First Edition

Britannica Educational Publishing
J. E. Luebering: Director, Core Reference Group
Anthony L. Green: Editor, Compton's by Britannica

Rosen Publishing
Hope Lourie Killcoyne: Executive Editor
Christine Poolos: Editor
Nelson Sá: Art Director
Nicole Russo: Designer
Cindy Reiman: Photography Manager

Cataloging-in-Publication Data

Crompton, Samuel Willard.
Discovering Ancient Rome/Samuel Willard Crompton.
     pages cm.—(Exploring ancient civilizations)
Includes bibliographical references and index.
ISBN 978-1-62275-840-1 (library bound)—ISBN 978-1-62275-839-5 (pbk.)—
ISBN 978-1-62275-838-8 (6-pack)
1. Rome—Juvenile literature. I. Title.
DG77.C68 2015
937—dc23
                                                                2014021752

Manufactured in the United States of America

Photo credits: Cover, pp. 1, 3 Phant/Shutterstock.com; pp. 6-7 cudak/Shutterstock.com; p. 9 Bridgeman Art Library, London/SuperStock; pp. 10, 15 De Agostini/SuperStock; p. 11 Private Collection/ The Stapleton Collection/Bridgeman Images; p. 13 Fine Art Images/SuperStock; p. 18 SF photo/ Shutterstock.com; p. 19 Stephen Alvarez/National Geographic Image Collection/Getty Images; p. 20 PeterHermesFurian/iStock/Thinkstock; p. 23 Culture Club/Hulton Archive/Getty Images; pp. 25, 28 © North Wind Picture Archives; p. 27 Dorling Kindersley/Thinkstock; p. 30 De Agostini Picture Library/ Bridgeman Images; p. 32 Duncan Walker/E+/Getty Images; p. 33 DEA/G. Dagli Orti/De Agostini/Getty Images; p. 36 The Bridgeman Art Library/Getty Images; p. 37 Stephen Finn/Shutterstock.com; p. 39 Danilo Ascione/Shutterstock.com; p. 42 Heritage Images/Hulton Fine Art Collection/Getty Images; p. 43 eFesenko/Shutterstock.com; cover and interior graphics © iStockphoto.com/pixonaut (patterned banners and borders), HorenkO/Shutterstock.com and Freckles/Shutterstock.com (background textures).

CONTENTS

When we think of Rome, we naturally visualize the Colosseum, the grandest of all Roman buildings. We also think of the Forum, the first and greatest of all government buildings that contributed to build our approach to modern democracy. Yet another image that comes to mind is of the aqueduct system, which brought fresh, clean water from the countryside. But when we think of the Roman people, we should, perhaps, be most impressed by their staying power. Rome was a republic for almost five hundred years and then an empire for another five hundred. No other people built so much or lasted so long at the top. How did they accomplish it?

This book treats ancient Rome in four distinct chapters. The first describes the rise of Rome, and the second its fall. The transition from kingdom to republic and from republic to empire is discussed. The third chapter examines how the Romans lived and how they experienced their world. And the fourth and final chapter tells how Rome's accomplishments continue to influence the world today. When all is said and done, the Romans will be revealed for what they really were: builders of our world.

The Forum was the center of Roman government, but it was also the center of the Roman world. Distances throughout the Roman Empire were measured by the miles that separated locations from the Forum.

CHAPTER ONE

FROM KINGDOM TO EMPIRE

R ome wasn't built in a day. In fact, it took about seven hundred years to progress from a small town on the Tiber River to an empire that straddled the entire Mediterranean world, meaning Italy, Greece, Egypt, and North Africa, as well as the many islands of that inland sea.

Myths and Legends

Romans felt they were special, right from the very beginning. One of their foundation stories, which is probably mythical, is that Aeneas—one of the princes of Troy—escaped the Greek destruction of his city and wandered for many years before founding the city of Rome. Another story is that two brothers, Romulus and Remus, who were raised by a she-wolf, founded Rome together.

During the early years, roughly 753–509 BCE, the Romans developed a complex religious belief system,

Romulus and Remus, raised by a she-wolf, were believed to be the founders of Rome. The city fathers marked the traditional date as 753 BCE.

based on the worship of many gods and goddesses. The gods and goddesses of ancient Rome were a jealous, envious, and rather human-like group. They fought each other frequently, and sometimes they involved humans in their quarrels.

Roman Government

The first settlers of Rome were people known as Latins. The area around Rome

HERCULES VS. MARS

One of the best-known quarrels in classical mythology was between Mars, the god of war, and Hercules. They fought many times, with Hercules usually the winner. The nastiest of their fights came when Hercules killed Mars's mortal son, Cycnus. Mars descended from the heavens to take revenge, but Hercules wounded him with a pitchfork.

Mars was the god of war, and, as such, he was worshipped by virtually all the leading politicians and generals. The city-state of Rome showed its martial prowess early on, and this only continued as the city-state evolved into a republic and, finally, an empire.

was called Latium. Sometime around 600 BCE, Rome was conquered by the Etruscans, a people to the north. Rome was then ruled by a series of Etruscan kings. But in 509 BCE, the Romans overthrew the last Etruscan monarch—Tarquin the Proud—and started a republic.

During the early years of the republic, Rome was small enough that the general body of the male citizens could be summoned whenever a major decision was needed. Over time, this became unworkable because the Roman population grew so rapidly. There just was not enough room for all the citizens to gather in one place. Once that level was reached, Rome became a representative republic, meaning that the citizens voted for men to represent them.

Developed over about two centuries, the Roman Republic was a clever combination of monarchy, aristocracy, and democracy. Two consuls— elected each year by a military body called the centuriate assembly (*comitia centuriata*)— were the chief executives of the republic. Rome believed in having two men at the top so that if one were injured or disabled, the other could fill his shoes. Imagine the United States having two presidents leading the country.

About three hundred senators—chosen through

These two consuls—coequal chief executives of the republic— are shadowed by servants carrying the fasces, or symbols of authority. The consuls—as well as senators and tribunes—were sacrosanct, meaning that no one could physically harm them, on pain of death.

family descent—acted as the legislature of Rome: they wrote the laws. During the early republic, the senators were elected, but over time it became obvious that men from the wealthiest upper-class families would win all the elections. A seat in the Senate was, therefore, made hereditary, staying within a family.

As many as ten tribunes—officials chosen on a yearly basis by the common citizens, known as plebeians or plebs—sat in the Senate and observed its debates. They did not have the power to debate the issues, or even to vote, but each tribune had the power to veto any acts of the Senate deemed unjust to any citizen, (*veto* means "I forbid").

Success in War

Between 509 and 202 BCE, Rome met a number of enemies. There were some defeats, as when the Gauls invaded from the north and briefly held Rome, in 390 BCE. Over time, however, Rome conquered the rest of Italy and Sicily. That conquest brought it into a life-or-death struggle with ancient Carthage, a city-state on the southern rim of the Mediterranean Sea. Carthage found a hero in the great general Hannibal, but Rome, with its system of government and a growing citizen-based army, eventually prevailed. When Carthage was completely destroyed, in 146 BCE, Rome was the sole ruler of the western Mediterranean, and soon it expanded its control to the eastern Mediterranean.

By about 133 BCE, Rome had entered a long period of unrest and civil war. Romans fought each other many times, but in 73–71 BCE they also had to put down a dangerous revolt of the slaves, led by a Thracian slave

Hannibal led the Carthaginian forces against Rome in the Second Punic War, one of three wars fought between Rome and Carthage during the second and third centuries BCE.

and gladiator named Spartacus. At the same time, the Romans were moving in a supremely practical direction. They were headed toward becoming an empire.

ROMAN LEGION

The Roman legion was a force of about six thousand men. At its best, the legion was almost unbeatable because of the discipline and commitment of its soldiers.

Julius Caesar

In 49 BCE, Julius Caesar, a very successful Roman army general, provoked a civil war by leading his forces, against orders from the Senate, across the river Rubicon, which marked the boundary between Italy and Caesar's province in Gaul. In the ensuing war, Caesar was pitted against Pompey, another very skillful Roman general, and Romans fought Romans in a terrible series of battles. Pompey fled from Italy but was pursued and defeated by Caesar at Pharsalus, in northern Greece, in 48 BCE. Pompey then fled to Egypt, where he was murdered. Having followed

Julius Caesar was attacked, stabbed, and killed by sixty senators who disapproved of his way of governing.

Pompey to Egypt, Caesar became lover to the queen Cleopatra and supported her militarily. He defeated Pompey's last supporters by 45 BCE and was subsequently named dictator for life by the Romans. Alarmed by Caesar's one-man rule, about sixty senators joined in a conspiracy to assassinate him. Caesar was stabbed to death in the Senate House at Rome on March 15, 44 BCE.

BEWARE THE IDES OF MARCH

Romans used the word *Ides* to mark the middle of the month. Because Caesar was killed on March 15, we have the expression, "Beware the Ides of March!"

Augustus Caesar

For a few years after Julius Caesar's death, it seemed as if Rome would remain a republic. The problems of poverty, unemployment, and homelessness grew even worse, however, and in 27 BCE, Augustus Caesar, who was both Julius Caesar's nephew and his adopted son, became the new leader of Rome. He, too, had fought and won a civil war, and when it was over, he was recognized as Rome's first citizen (*princeps civitatis*).

Augustus never called himself emperor. He knew too well what had happened to his famous uncle. But over the next thirty years, he turned Rome into what was effectively an empire. And when he died, in 14 CE, his stepson and successor, Tiberius, did indeed call himself emperor.

The ancient city of Rome was now the center of one of the largest and most powerful empires the world had ever seen.

CHAPTER TWO
FROM EMPIRE TO DUST

Rome peaked around the year 100 CE. At that time, there were about one million people in the city and another seventy million throughout the empire. This area now extended from what Romans called the Pillars of Hercules (and what we call the Strait of Gibraltar) to Palestine in the east. Such a collection of peoples, languages, and cultures had never previously existed under one rule.

The Early Emperors

Although each one of them carried the name of "Caesar," none of the emperors who came after Julius Caesar and Augustus Caesar were as strong or effective as the two originals. Luckily, however, these early Roman emperors received a foundation so strong that it could endure almost any problem.

Tiberius was followed by Caligula, Claudius, and then Nero. None of these men had an especially good reputation, but historians believe that Caligula was the worst of the lot. He suffered a severe illness seven months into his rule and became mentally unstable, acting unpredictably and often cruelly toward his subjects. The Romans soon grew weary of his tyrannical rule, and a group of conspirators assassinated him after he had reigned for only four years. Nero was the last ruler in the line descended from Julius Caesar. For two years after Nero's death, there were struggles for the throne, but after Vespasian was proclaimed emperor in 69 CE, the government stabilized.

The Colosseum is the grandest of all visible remains of ancient Rome. It was so well designed that the fifty thousand spectators could rapidly be evacuated in case of a fire, or, as the Romans often feared, an earthquake.

The Colosseum was completed around 80 CE, and the Pantheon—Rome's most beautiful temple, which was been begun in 27 BCE by the statesman Marcus Vispanius Agrippa—was rebuilt by the emperor Hadrian sometime between 118 and 128 CE. Augustus Caesar liked to claim that he found Rome a city of stone and left her one of marble, but, in truth, it took another century after his death to complete the process.

The *Pax Romana*

By about 100 CE, Rome had filled out, geographically, militarily, and culturally. Latin was the first language of the Romans and Italians and the second language everywhere else in the Mediterranean world. The Spaniards, Jews,

Among the most notable of ancient Rome's public works is the huge sewer Cloaca Maxima, which is still in use today.

North Africans, Greeks, Bulgarians, Britons, Gauls, and others were now under Roman rule. There were benefits involved, and these increased when one became a full-fledged Roman citizen. Many people, throughout the empire, agreed that life under Rome was rather good. The rule of law prevailed, both in the Eternal City and in the provinces.

Pax Romana means "the Roman Peace," which prevailed everywhere from about 100 to 190. During those three or four generations, there was little, if any, warfare in

At its maximum extent, the Roman Empire completely covered the Mediterranean world, Egypt, and much of the Middle East. The same language, laws, and customs prevailed throughout this vast area, making Rome's achievement far more than just a military one.

the Roman world. The Roman legions kept the peace; Roman governors administered the laws; and Roman priests infiltrated the provinces, bringing with them the Roman religion.

The seventy million people who lived under the rule of Rome never came to love the Romans, but many came to admire what Rome brought. Peace, prosperity, and a general sense of well-being pervaded the Roman Empire during the *Pax Romana*. Some historians believe that these three or four generations represent the single

ROMAN GODS

During the *Pax Romana*, the different Roman emperors were worshipped as gods. They did not replace any of the early gods; rather, they took their place alongside them.

happiest time of recorded human history. The good times did not last though.

The Walls Begin to Crumble

Starting around 195, the Roman Empire began to be ruled by lesser men. Neither as committed nor as courageous as the earlier emperors, these men increasingly became weak, corrupt, and selfish. To be sure, all of the problems that came upon Rome cannot be blamed on the third-century emperors. The empire had grown so large, encompassing so many peoples, that it was difficult to rule. Also, it became hard for the emperor, in Rome, to know whether he was told the truth about what happened in the many provinces. As a result, the military fortunes of the empire began to wane.

The Rise of Christianity

Although Christianity began with the ministry of Jesus of Nazareth in the first century, it remained a minority religion within the Roman Empire for several more centuries. Over time, as the old Roman polytheistic religion proved increasingly unpopular, millions of people throughout the empire began to turn to Christianity. This should not have been a negative, but some of the emperors took it as one.

During the rule of Emperor Diocletian, in the late third century, Christians were actively persecuted, and many were killed. Only during the reign of the Emperor Constantine, who was Diocletian's successor, did the Roman government begin to grant important freedoms and concessions to the church. Constantine himself converted to Christianity, and in 313 he issued the Edict of Milan, giving Christians the right to practice their religion openly. By the end of the fourth century, Christianity had been transformed from a small persecuted sect to the dominant faith of the empire.

Constantine is also remembered for moving the seat of government from Rome to the east. He moved the capital to the ancient Greek city of Byzantium on the Black Sea by 330 and renamed it Constantinople (the city is now Istanbul, Turkey). After the move, Rome steadily declined while the Eastern Roman, or Byzantine, Empire lasted for another thousand years.

This fresco of Jesus Christ comes from Rome, during the early Christian era.

Barbarian Conquests

During the fourth century, barbarian raids turned into barbarian invasions. The Goths, Vandals, Franks, Lombards, and others pressed in on the northern boundaries of the empire. All paled in comparison to the Huns, who came in the mid-fifth century.

Led by King Attila, the Huns pressed against the empire. Rome had already been sacked once—by the Goths in 410—and it seemed likely it would fall to Attila and his Huns. Instead, Rome was saved by what many Christians believed to be a miracle. Pope Leo the Great went north to meet Attila, and, though no one recorded their conversation, the Huns turned away from what would have been a terrible conquest and the sacking of Rome.

In 476, a barbarian leader named Odoacer entered Rome. There was practically no

ROME'S SHRINKING POPULATION

There were one million Romans in 100 CE, and only fifty thousand by 476. Some were killed, but far more fled, into the countryside, to escape by ship, and even to move to Constantinople.

resistance. Odoacer did not destroy Rome, but he did depose Romulus Augustulus, last of the Western Roman emperors. Although Rome was still a city, it had shrunk to a population of less than fifty thousand. As for the great Roman Empire, it was no more.

Romulus Augustulus, the last emperor in the Western Roman Empire, hands over his crown to Odoacer, leader of the Gothic tribes that had just conquered Rome.

CHAPTER THREE
HOW THE ROMANS LIVED

D ay-to-day life in ancient Rome was decidedly uneven. Men and women at the top of the social ladder lived very well indeed, while members of the fragile middle class managed to get by, even if just barely. For the people at the bottom of the social scale—the slaves especially—life was often miserable.

Patricians and Plebeians

Right from the start, Roman society was divided into two groups, the patricians and the plebeians. The patricians were those who claimed descent from the earliest Roman families. They could trace, they said, their bloodlines right back to the time when Rome was founded.

The plebeians were the workers and common citizens. Perhaps they could not afford to pay scholars to verify their bloodlines. Then again, they may not have cared to do so. The result was that Rome had an aristocracy, made up of those whose families had

Ancient Rome had a rigid class system, with patricians (*left*) and plebeians (*right*), who formed the working class. There were also soldiers and slaves (*center*).

lived in the city a long time, and a working class, composed of almost everyone else.

Being a patrician did not necessarily mean a person was rich, but over time the two things began to seem like the same. Being of plebeian

CAESAR'S BLOODLINE

Julius Caesar was, naturally, quite concerned about his bloodline. Over time, he hired scholars and genealogists who claimed he was descended from one of the first settlers of Rome.

birth, on the other hand, often meant that one was poor, and this, too, became even more likely with the passage of time.

Servants and Slaves

In the early republic, there were aristocrats, merchants, workers, and quite a few servants. A man or a woman might serve a rich family

A patrician man is carried by footmen.

for his or her whole life, yet still be seen as a free person. This changed with the Roman wars, which brought slaves to Rome.

Between about 202 BCE—with the end of the Second Punic War—and 44 BCE—the year when Julius Caesar was assassinated—hundreds of thousands of slaves were brought to Rome. Victorious generals dragged conquered people in huge groups to Rome, where they were sold on the auction block as slaves. Not all of them remained in the city. Many were made to farm the Italians' lands. To some extent, Rome flourished because of the work of these slaves.

ROMAN AQUEDUCTS

Clean water was supplied to the city of Rome by an impressive system of aqueducts. Construction of the aqueducts was carried out by slaves, paid laborers, and the Roman army legions. Around Rome, eleven major aqueducts were built over a period of more than five hundred years. The first one, the Aqua Appia, was built in 312 BCE and was 10 miles (16 kilometers) long. The last, the Aqua Alexandrina, was built in about 226 CE. The longest was the 58-mile (93 km) Aqua Marcia, built in 144 BCE. The Romans also built aqueducts in many other parts of their empire.

Figs, Olives, and Grapes

Upper-class Romans lived a very fine lifestyle, particularly where food was concerned. Italy had plenty of native foods, many of them picked or harvested by slaves, but there was, throughout Italy, an increasing use of foreign foods. The wheat used to make Italian bread came primarily from

Upper-class Romans enjoyed seemingly never-ending, sumptuous feasts. This fresco depicts Julius Caesar at the height of his power, receiving the annual tax arriving from Egypt. Caesar and Augustus formulated the system under which Egyptian wealth—grain in particular—formed the basis for the "bread and circuses" offered in Rome.

Egypt, and the best grapes usually were from Greece. Italian farmers cultivated fig trees, but the finest figs came from North Africa, as did the animals that were slaughtered to provide meat. With the addition of an interest in producing fine wine, virtually all the ingredients for a truly superior diet were available to wealthy Romans.

Bread and Circuses

The food consumed by the upper-class Romans was readily available, in part because the buyers made arrangements with farmers and middlemen. The same was not true for much of the rest of the Roman population. The poor were able to afford only very basic foodstuffs. Over time, Roman emperors developed the custom of providing free bread to the public, as well as circuses, or entertainment.

Romans had liked to watch armed combat for generations, but the gladiator contests that we think of today began in earnest in the first century BCE. When the Colosseum was completed and opened to the public, gladiators fought on a regular basis. They fought each other with pitchfork and

The victorious gladiator looks up to the stands to ask whether the defeated man shall live or die. The crowd would make its opinion known, through cheers or boos, and the emperor would then give a "thumbs up" or a "thumbs down."

sword; they fought animals with spears and axes; and the Colosseum was even flooded at times so the gladiators could fight naval battles, with tiny ships.

No one knows how many slaves, gladiators, and Christians were "fed to the lions," as the expression goes, but it was, very likely, in the tens of thousands. The Colosseum was open for more than three hundred years, and the Roman public went, day after day, to see men and beasts tear each other apart.

Teachers and Tutors

Throughout its long history, Rome never equaled Greece in the fine arts. There were good Roman poets and philosophers and excellent architects and designers, but nearly everyone recognized that Greece remained number one. For that reason, upper-class Romans often brought teachers and tutors from Greece, in order that their children might become more refined and sophisticated.

This relief depicts a teacher—who is almost certainly Greek—instructing his Roman students. Latin was the language of government, law, and business, while Greek was the language of art, philosophy, and poetry.

Upper-class Roman boys learned Latin and Greek, plain mathematics, and mathematical theory. They learned how to recite from Homer, Virgil, and a dozen other famous poets. Roman girls, however, generally did not receive a formal education, though sometimes young girls were allowed to attend elementary school, known as the *ludus publicus*. After having completed elementary school, boys of the upper classes usually attended a grammar school, and at age sixteen, boys who wanted training for public service went on to study public speaking at the rhetoric schools.

The graded arrangement of schools established in Rome by the middle of the first century BCE ultimately spread throughout the Roman Empire. It continued until the fall of the empire in the fifth century CE.

CHAPTER FOUR

ROME'S LEGACY

Rome was clearly one of the great builders of Western civilization. Today, the inhabitants of the Western world have much to thank Rome for.

Government

Several aspects of modern government can be traced directly to ancient Rome. For example, in the United States, the president can cast a veto—derived from the Roman vetoes, cast by the tribunes. So can the governors of the individual states. In the U.S. system and also in other modern constitutional systems, a separation of powers exists—the division of the executive, legislative, and judicial functions of government into separate and independent bodies—so that no one branch of government can completely dominate the others. This idea, too, is taken in part from Rome.

Rome also provided a powerful example of the ability of government to act for the good of society. The Romans were gifted city planners. Rome's roads were without match in the ancient world, designed

This artwork, *The Barbarians Before Rome*, depicts one of many invasions and raids to the former Roman Empire by barbarians.

for comparatively fast transportation and adapted to a wide variety of functions: commerce, agriculture, mail delivery, pedestrian traffic, and military movements. In addition, Roman city planners contributed to public health with their extensive networks of sewers, aqueducts that provided clean water, and systems that drained waste water from public baths.

In Roman times, the government also ensured justice and security for millions of people. In our time, governments enforce many regulations that have been created on

The Roman aqueduct system brought fresh water to the city of Rome for centuries. Even today, parts of the system survive, a testament to the skill of Roman architects and builders.

the behalf of every person. Lacking such protections, we would live in a state of anarchy.

The proof of this is seen when we look at the Early Middle Ages. The Roman Empire ceased to exist in 476 CE, and the Western world endured a series of barbarian invasions and raids. The tribespeople who conquered Rome did not know how to employ the techniques and tools of civilization. The aqueduct system, for example, fell into ruins. About the only remnant of Roman civilization that was still visible in the countryside was the network of Roman roads, many of which remain today.

CODE OF JUSTINIAN

The most complete and complex system of laws in the ancient world was developed by the Romans. It was the product of many centuries of civilization, from the early years of the republic until the end of the empire. In the sixth century BCE, the Byzantine emperor Justinian I collected and organized these laws. The resulting Code of Justinian included collections of past laws and extracts of the opinions of the great Roman jurists. Also included were an elementary outline of Roman law and a collection of Justinian's new laws.

Law

Roman law has strongly influenced the development of legal systems in virtually every country of the Western world as well as in parts of the East. It forms the basis for the modern law codes of most countries of continental Europe and systems based on them elsewhere.

During the history of the Roman Empire, Roman law spread to every corner of the Mediterranean world. The Romans did not have a jury system such as we have today. Rather, an all-powerful judge heard testimony from both sides and rendered his decision.

The various Roman laws and the legal interpretations that had been handed down were all finally codified in the sixth century CE and became known as the Code of Justinian.

National Boundaries

When Rome was a small city-state, there were few, if any, national boundaries in the Mediterranean world (Egypt was one of the rare exceptions to this rule). By the time Rome became a powerful empire, the national and ethnic boundaries were much more obvious and secure. A Gaul could not be

A section of Roman road still survives today. Rome built its famous roads to speed the legions on their way, but the solidity of these roads helped in other ways, such as the delivery of goods across Italy.

MONASTIC TRADITION

The Christian monastic tradition began in the second century CE, but it took on greater life with the writing of a series of monastic rules. Saint Benedict of Nursia, who ran the monastery at Monte Cassino, about 100 miles (160 km) south of Rome, was responsible for it.

confused for a German, and a Spaniard was clearly not a North African or a Greek. The long period of the Roman Empire allowed ethnic and national boundaries to become much clearer and more distinct.

Learning

When the Roman Empire fell, virtually all of the learning and knowledge known to the Romans was written either in Latin or in Greek. Over the next two or three generations, much knowledge was lost forever. Sometimes it was burned by barbarian tribespeople; at other times it simply fell victim to disuse. But a substantial portion of Greek and Latin writing was preserved by the Christian monks, and it is no accident that much of it happened in Italy.

Language

Latin, the language of the Romans, became the medium for a significant body of original works in Western civilization. The speeches of the great Roman orator Cicero, the histories of Livy and Tacitus, and above all the poetry of Virgil are all part of the legacy of Rome.

The lasting effects of Roman rule in Europe can also be seen in the widespread use of the Romance languages, including Italian, French, Spanish, Portuguese, and Romanian. All these languages evolved from Latin. The Western alphabet of twenty-six letters is another example of the cultural legacy that Rome left to Western civilization.

Food and Entertainment

Some historians claim that all of us in the Western world are Romans today. They mean that we follow many of the ideas of what the Romans considered the good life.

To the Romans, good food was almost synonymous with good living. They did overdo it sometimes, with their five-course meals. In entertainment, too, we are very like the Romans. When one examines the Colosseum—which has in large part survived—one sees many similarities between it and the American football stadiums of today, including the oval shape, methods of entry, and seating design. Though some people criticize American football for being too violent, it is, at least, not a fight to the death like the old gladiatorial shows.

Formal schooling in ancient Rome was available to those who could afford to pay. While both boys and girls could attend school, they were usually educated separately and taught different things. Girls were less likely to focus on scholarly or vocational pursuits and instead were encouraged to focus on family.

Empire or Republic?

Finally, perhaps most important, Rome gave to us today a divided legacy in terms of government. For almost five hundred years, Rome was a fully functioning republic, with consuls, senators, tribunes, and censors. After that, Rome turned into an empire that lasted for nearly five hundred more years. This empire had one man at the top, and a huge number of bureaucrats beneath him. Many experts acknowledge that the Roman Empire was a rather inefficient organization.

This modern-day scene is from a street in a Greek city. The Roman arch suggests that Rome's influence can still be found in our modern world.

Today, people of the Western world struggle with the same fluctuation between republic and empire. Americans, for example, are very concerned with being a democratic people, yet at times it seems the United States veers close to an empire in the eyes of the world. In this, as in so many other ways, people still look to Rome both for guidance and for warning.

Lasting Legacy

Rome was the city that became a city-state that conquered the entire Mediterranean world. For almost five hundred years, it presided over that world, shaping it and providing instruction for all those who came later. The city fell to the barbarians, and the empire ceased to exist, but the ideas and ideals upon which both the city and the empire were built can still be felt and experienced today.

GLOSSARY

ANARCHY Lack of government; everyone does as they wish.

ARISTOCRACY The rule of a group of people who form an upper class based on money and social status.

BARBARIAN In ancient Rome, this referred to almost anyone who did not speak Latin.

CAESAR Originally the family name of Julius Caesar, it was used by all the emperors of Rome.

DEMOCRACY A form of government in which people choose leaders by voting.

EMPIRE A group of countries or regions that are controlled by one ruler or one government.

EXECUTIVE The executive branch of government determines and directs government policy; it is where some of the most important decisions—often having to do with war and peace, life and death—are made.

GLADIATOR A man in ancient Rome who fought against another man or animal for public entertainment.

GOTH A member of a Germanic people that overran the Roman Empire in the early centuries of the Christian era.

HUN A member of a nomadic central Asian people who gained control of a large part of central and eastern Europe under Attila about 450 CE.

LEGISLATURE The body of officials chosen by the people to make the laws.

MONARCHY The rule of one person who is called a king, queen, or emperor.

MONASTIC There are many monastic traditions around the world; the Christian form centers around monks or nuns living together in religious community.

MYTHICAL A story based on an oral tradition, the source of which is sometimes doubtful.

PATRICIAN A member of one of the original citizen families of ancient Rome.

PAX ROMANA Literally "the Roman Peace," which ran from about 100 to 195 CE.

PLEBEIAN Common person of ancient Rome.

POLYTHEISTIC The worship of many gods and goddesses.

REPUBLIC A country that is governed by elected representatives and by an elected leader (such as a president) rather than by a king or a queen.

ROMANCE LANGUAGES Those present-day languages that share common roots in Latin.

TRIBUNE In ancient Rome, an official who guarded the interest of the plebeian class.

Benoit, Peter. *Ancient Rome.* New York, NY: Children's Press, 2012.

Bingham, Jane. *How People Lived in Ancient Rome.* New York, NY: Rosen Publishing, 2009.

DiPrimio, Pete. *How'd They Do That? In Ancient Rome.* Hockessin, DE: Mitchell Lane Publishers, 2010.

Dubois, Muriel L. *Ancient Rome: A Mighty Empire.* North Mankato, MN: Capstone Press, 2011.

Fowler, Will. *The Story of Ancient Weapons.* New York, NY: Rosen Publishing, 2011.

Malam, John. *Life in Ancient Rome.* North Mankato, MN: Capstone Press, 2010.

Platt, Richard, et al. *Roman Diary: The Journal of Iliona of Mytilini, Who Was Captured by Pirates and Sold as a Slave in Rome, AD 107.* Somerville, MA: Candlewick Press, 2009.

Steele, Philip. *The Roman Empire: Passport to the Past.* New York, NY: Rosen Publishing, 2009.

Websites

Because of the changing nature of Internet links, Rosen Publishing has developed an online list of websites related to the subject of this book. This site is updated regularly. Please use this link to access the list:

http://www.rosenlinks.com/ANCIV/Rome

FOR MORE INFORMATION

A

aqueduct system, 6, 29, 36, 37
aristocracy, 11, 26–27, 28
army, 12–13, 14, 29

B

barbarians, conquest of Rome
  by, 24–25, 37, 40, 43
Byzantium (Constantinople),
  23, 24

C

Caesar, Augustus, 16, 17, 19
Caesar, Julius, 14–15, 16, 17, 18,
  27, 29
Caligula, 17–18
Carthage, 12–13
Christianity, 22–23
Christians, 24, 32, 40
  acceptance of, 23
  persecution of, 22
circuses, 31–32
Cleopatra, 14–15
Code of Justinian, 38, 39
Colosseum, 6, 19, 31–32, 41
conquests of Rome, 12–13,
  19–20
Constantine, 22–23
consuls, 11, 42

D

democracy, 6, 11, 43
Diocletian, 22–23

E

education, 33–34
emperors, 16, 17, 18, 19, 21–23, 25,
  31, 38
empire, 6, 29, 34, 37, 38, 39, 40
  distinction between republic,
    42–43
  end of, 21–25
  life in, 20–21, 26, 41
  peak of, 17–21
  problems of, 21–22
  progression to, 8–16
entertainment, 31, 41

F

food, 30–31, 41

G

Gauls, 12, 19–20, 39–40
gladiators, 13–14, 31–32
  contests, 31, 41
government, 9–12, 18, 22–23,
  35–37, 42

H

Hannibal, 12–13

K

kingdom, 6
  progression from, 8–16